A Life Full of Forbearance but without Anxiety

D0615852

Witness Lee

Living Stream Ministry
Anaheim, California • www.lsm.org

Mass-distribution Edition, August 2011.

ISBN 978-0-7363-4631-3

Free distribution by:
Bibles for America
P. O. Box 17537, Irvine, CA 92623 U.S.A.

See back page for local distribution information.

Published by:
Living Stream Ministry
2431 W. La Palma Ave., Anaheim, CA 92801 U.S.A.
P. O. Box 2121, Anaheim, CA 92814 U.S.A.

Printed in the United States of America

CONTENTS

PREFACE

All the New Testament writings have a doctrinal ingredient. But strictly speaking, Philippians is not concerned with doctrine; it is concerned with the experience of Christ.

Concerning the experience of Christ, each chapter of Philippians covers a major point. First, in chapter one we have the magnification of Christ. No matter what the circumstances are in which we find ourselves, we need to express Christ in such a way that we magnify Him. In chapter two Paul presents Christ as our pattern. In everything we do, we need a pattern, a model, an example. Even in the experience of Christ and the enjoyment of Christ, we need a pattern. This pattern is Christ Himself. Chapter three indicates that Christ should be our goal, our aim. We who love the Lord and seek Him are not aimless. Our aim is Christ Himself. He is the goal toward which we press. Finally, in chapter four, Christ is our strength. In 4:13 Paul says, "I can do all things in Him who empowers me." Christ is not only the pattern and the goal; He is also the strength, the power, the dynamo. As the dynamo within us, He empowers us to live Him, to magnify Him, and to press on toward Him as the goal. In the four chapters of Philippians we see Christ as the One lived out and magnified, Christ as the pattern, Christ as the goal, and Christ as our inward strength. This book on the experience of Christ covers four major points: the expression, the pattern, the goal, and the strength. We all need to experience Christ in this fourfold way.

In Philippians 4:5-9 Paul speaks of the excellent characteristics in our living which are the issue of our experience of Christ, including things that are true, things that are dignified, things that are righteous, things that are pure, things that are lovely, and things that are well spoken of. All of these characteristics come out of a life that is full of forbearance but without anxiety.

Forbearance is Christ as our living. Forbearance is actually a synonym for Christ in our Christian living. On the one hand, we may say that our Christian life is Christ. On the other hand, we may say that the Christian life is a life of forbearance. To make our forbearance known, therefore, means to make our Christ known. If we do not make known our forbearance, we will have Christ only in doctrine, but not in our experience. To let our forbearance be made known is to make known to others the Christ whom we experience, live, and magnify.

A life full of forbearance but without anxiety is the focus of the chapters contained in this publication. These chapters were given in 1980 by Witness Lee as the concluding seven messages in the *Life-study of Philippians*. An outline of the book of Philippians and information on all sixty-two messages in this Life-study series are also included in this publication.

THE EPISTLE OF PAUL TO THE PHILIPPIANS

OUTLINE

I. Introduction—1:1-2

II. Living Christ to magnify Him—1:3-30
   A. Fellowship for the furtherance of the gospel—vv. 3-18
   B. Magnifying Christ by living Him—vv. 19-26
   C. Striving along with the gospel with one soul—vv. 27-30

III. Taking Christ as the pattern and holding Him forth—2:1-30
   A. Joined in soul, thinking the one thing—vv. 1-4
   B. Taking Christ as the pattern—vv. 5-11
   C. Working out our salvation to hold forth Christ—vv. 12-16
   D. A drink offering upon the sacrifice of faith—vv. 17-18
   E. The apostle's concern for the believers—vv. 19-30

IV. Pursuing Christ to gain Him—3:1-21
   A. Serving by the Spirit and not trusting in the flesh—vv. 1-6
   B. Counting all things loss on account of Christ—vv. 7-11
   C. Gaining Christ by pursuing Him—vv. 12-16
   D. Awaiting Christ for the transfiguration of the body—vv. 17-21

V. Having Christ as the secret of sufficiency—4:1-20
   A. Thinking the same thing and rejoicing in the Lord—vv. 1-4
   B. Excellent characteristics in living—vv. 5-9
   C. The believers' fellowship with the apostle and the apostle's secret of sufficiency—vv. 10-20

VI. Conclusion—4:21-23

CHAPTER ONE

A LIFE FULL OF FORBEARANCE
BUT WITHOUT ANXIETY

(1)

Scripture Reading: Phil. 4:1-7; 1:8; 2 Cor. 10:1a

In our reading of the book of Philippians it may seem that Paul's thought in 4:1-7 is not nearly as high as that expressed in the first three chapters. In chapter one he speaks of living Christ and magnifying Him; in chapter two, of taking Christ as our pattern, of shining as lights in the world, and of holding forth the word of life; and in chapter three, of the excellency of the knowledge of Christ and of pursuing toward the goal for the prize of the high calling of God in Christ Jesus. Then in chapter four Paul uses expressions that apparently are quite ordinary: "Rejoice in the Lord"; "Let your forbearance be known to all men"; and "In nothing be anxious." Suppose as you are pursuing toward the goal for the prize someone suddenly encouraged you not to be anxious. Would you not consider this an interruption and say, "I am pursuing Christ. I want to arrive at the goal of the out-resurrection. Why do you talk to me about anxiety?" Many readers of Philippians treasure the first three chapters, but, perhaps unconsciously, they may consider chapter four to be on a lower level than chapters one through three.

Years ago I appreciated the first three chapters of Philippians much more than I appreciated chapter four. It seemed to me that after ascending a high peak in chapters one, two, and three, Paul suddenly came down to a lower level in chapter four. I could not understand why there was such a sudden change in Paul's writing.

THE NEED TO LEARN THE SECRET

In 4:12 Paul says, "I have learned the secret." To do the things spoken of in chapter four requires the divine life. Paul had learned the secret of being able to do all things in the One who empowered him. In verse 4 he exhorts us to rejoice in the Lord always. We may think that it is easy to rejoice in the Lord. Actually, rejoicing in Him requires the out-resurrection. In order to rejoice in the Lord we need to be in Him as the One who empowers us. Thus, even the apparently simple matter of rejoicing in the Lord requires that we learn the secret. If we do not know the secret, we shall not be able to rejoice.

In 4:5 Paul says, "Let your forbearance be known to all men." In 2 Corinthians 10:1 he says, "I beseech you through the meekness and forbearance of Christ" (lit.). The forbearance mentioned in 4:5 is not an ordinary forbearance or an ethical forbearance. It is the forbearance of Christ, a spiritual attribute or a virtue of Christ. This forbearance must become our forbearance, and then we should make our forbearance, the forbearance of Christ, known to all men.

What is the meaning of forbearance, and why does Paul mention forbearance in 4:5 instead of some other virtue? If Paul had told us to let our love or kindness be made known to all men, this verse would not be a problem to us. But here Paul does not speak of love, kindness, humility, or some other human virtue. Instead, he singles out forbearance. We know what love, kindness, and humility are, but who can give an adequate definition of forbearance? If I had been asked years ago to define forbearance, I would have said that to forbear means to carry a heavy burden for a long period of time. However, this definition is natural. It does not help us to understand why Paul speaks of forbearance in 4:5 instead of some other virtue.

After telling us to let our forbearance be known to all men, Paul goes on to say, also in verse 5, "The Lord is near." Many expositors think that this means that the coming of the Lord is at hand. I dare not say that this meaning is not included; however, here Paul does not say that the Lord is coming soon, but that He is near already. Then in the next verse Paul tells us not to be anxious in anything, but "in everything, by prayer and petition with thanksgiving" to make our requests known to God. In the midst of making our forbearance known to all men, in not being anxious in anything, but in everything making our requests known to God, Paul declares that the Lord is near.

In ourselves, we are not able to make our forbearance known to all men, to be free from anxiety, or even to make our requests known to God. Some may think that it is easy to pray; actually, prayer is a difficult thing. In order to do all these things we, like Paul, must learn the secret. We also need to be in the One who empowers us.

STANDING FIRM IN THE LORD

Philippians 4:1-7 is part of Paul's concluding word to chapters one, two, and three. What he says in 4:1-7 is based on what he has previously written about living Christ, magnifying Christ, taking Christ as our pattern, knowing the excellency of Christ, pursuing toward the goal, and living in the out-resurrection.

In 4:1 he says, "So then, my brothers, beloved and longed for, my joy and crown, so stand firm in the Lord, beloved." We know from chapter three that Paul aspired to be found in Christ. In 4:1 he tells us to stand firm in the Lord. Standing firm in the Lord is the key to letting our forbearance be known to all men. If we do not stand firm in the Lord, there is no way to make our forbearance known. In order to do anything we must have a proper standing. This is true of making known our forbearance. For this, we must stand firm in the Lord; that is, we must remain in Him. Hence, Paul's word about standing firm in the Lord is equal to the Lord's word about abiding in Him (John 15:4).

In Philippians 4:2 Paul goes on to say, "I beseech Euodias, and I beseech Syntyche, to think the same thing in the Lord." As those who stand firm in the Lord, we should also "think the same thing in the Lord." Apart from the Lord, we cannot think the same thing. If we would think the same thing in the Lord, we must first stand firm in Him.

Verse 3 continues, "Yes, I ask you also, genuine yokefellow, assist them, who contended with me in the gospel, with both Clement and the rest of my fellow-workers, whose names are in the book of life." Here Paul is asking those who were genuine yokefellows to help Euodias and Syntyche to think the same thing. Paul seems to be saying, "These two sisters are my co-workers, but at least temporarily they are not in the Lord. I encourage you, genuine yokefellow, to do your best to bring them back to the Lord and help them to think the same thing in the Lord." These sisters were co-workers who had labored with Paul and contended with him in the gospel and whose names were in the book of life. Nevertheless, for the time being they were not in the Lord.

In verse 4 Paul says, "Rejoice in the Lord always; again I will say, rejoice." When in our experience we are not in the Lord, we do not have any joy and we cannot rejoice. Formerly Euodias and Syntyche could rejoice, but now, because they are not in the Lord, they cannot rejoice in Him.

There is a practical way by which we can know whether or not we are in the Lord. As long as you are not one with a certain brother or sister in the church, you are not in the Lord. Of course, as far as position is concerned, you are in Christ eternally. Nothing can affect our position in Christ. But practically and experientially we may not remain in Him. The fact that we are not one with a particular saint proves that we are not in the Lord.

It is very serious not to be one with even one brother or sister. Most of the saints have at least one other saint with whom they are not one. For example, suppose some sisters are serving together at a love feast. One sister may not like the way another sister is serving and she may refuse to serve with her. She may even walk away from this sister. By walking away from the sister, she actually walks out of the Lord. Instead of refusing to serve with the sister, she should make her forbearance known in that situation.

It is not easy to serve with the saints in the church. If an employee in a factory does not do a good job, the boss can fire him. But in the church life no one is hired and no one can be fired. Just as we have been born into a family and cannot be fired from being a member of the family, so we have been born into the church and cannot be fired from being a member of the church. When difficulties arise, we should not walk away from the saints or refuse to serve with them. Instead, we should exercise our forbearance.

NO ANXIETY

If we exercise forbearance, we shall not be anxious. Whenever we make our forbearance known, our anxiety is crossed out. When we exercise forbearance, we can rejoice in the Lord, and when we rejoice in the Lord, our anxiety disappears. Thus, forbearance maintains our rejoicing, and rejoicing drives away our anxiety. But whenever we do not exercise forbearance, we are not able to rejoice. Then the way is open for anxiety to enter in. This is not a mere doctrine; it is a word which touches the actual situation of our Christian life.

SATISFIED WITH LESS THAN OUR DUE

At this point we need to consider in a fuller way the meaning of forbearance. Forbearance means that we are easily satisfied, even with less than our due. This is the meaning of the Greek word rendered *forbearance*. To be satisfied with less than our due is in contrast to being just in an exacting way. To forbear is to make no demands on others; it is to be satisfied with whatever another party does to us or for us. Suppose a brother's wife serves him a cold drink when he preferred a hot one, and, very dissatisfied, he rebukes her for what she has done. This is not forbearance; it is being just in a very exacting manner. If the brother had shown forbearance toward his wife, he would have been satisfied with whatever she served him, even if he had not been able to drink it. He would have been satisfied with less than his due.

AN ALL-INCLUSIVE VIRTUE

In his *Word Studies* Wuest points out that the Greek word rendered *forbearance* not only means satisfied with less than our due, but also means sweet reasonableness. The word includes self-control, patience, moderation, kindness, and gentleness. Furthermore, according to Christian experience, forbearance is all-inclusive, for it includes all Christian virtues. This means that if we fail to exercise forbearance, we fail to exercise any Christian virtue. If a brother's wife serves him a cold drink contrary to his preference and he complains about it, then at that time he does not exhibit any Christian virtue. But if by the grace of Christ he is satisfied with less than his due and exercises forbearance toward his wife, not criticizing her or condemning her, he will show in his forbearance an all-inclusive Christian virtue. His forbearance will include patience, humility, self-control, looking to the Lord, and even the virtue of admitting that the Lord is sovereign in all things.

The reason we sometimes behave in an unseemly manner is that we lack forbearance. Negative attitudes and unkind words also come from a shortage of forbearance. When we fail to love, it is because we have no forbearance. Likewise, we may be intolerant because we lack forbearance. Even talkativeness may result from having no forbearance. If we do not have forbearance, we shall not have peace. If we do not show forbearance toward the members of our family, there will be no peace in our family life. Peace comes out of forbearance.

MAGNIFYING CHRIST BY MAKING KNOWN OUR FORBEARANCE

Paul realized that forbearance is an all-inclusive virtue. This is the reason he says, "Let your forbearance be known to all men." This forbearance is actually Christ Himself. In 1:21 Paul says, "To me to live is Christ." Since Christ is forbearance, for Paul to live was forbearance. Paul's earnest expectation was that Christ would be magnified in him, whether through life or through death. For Paul to magnify Christ was for him to make known his forbearance. Thus, for Christ to be magnified in us is equal to making our forbearance known to all men. The reason for this is that forbearance is Christ experienced by us in a practical way. We may speak of living Christ and testify that for us to live is Christ. However, day by day in our life at home what we need is forbearance. If we have forbearance, then in our experience we truly have Christ. If a brother's wife offends him, what he needs to make known to her is Christ as his forbearance.

It is very difficult to be a good husband or wife. The key to being a good husband or wife is forbearance. To repeat, forbearance includes much more than gentleness or humility. As an all-inclusive Christian virtue, forbearance is Christ Himself. In both the family life and in the church life, we need to live Christ by living a life of forbearance.

The more we consider the significance of forbearance, the more we can appreciate why Paul spoke of it in 4:5. Our failures and defeats in the Christian life come because we are short of forbearance. All the saints, young and old alike, have a tendency to neglect forbearance. If we would live Christ, we must be satisfied with less than our due. We should not make exacting demands on others.

The Lord Jesus lived a life of forbearance when He was on earth. In one sense, He was very strict, but in another sense He was very tolerant. For example, although He prayed a great deal, He did not make demands of His disciples concerning prayer or condemn them because they did not pray enough.

THE NEARNESS OF THE LORD

Immediately after speaking about forbearance, Paul goes on to say, "The Lord is near." As I have indicated, I do not oppose the understanding that this refers to the nearness of the Lord's coming. Nevertheless, according to experience, not according to doctrine, I would say that this word refers to the Lord's presence with us today. It also strengthens Paul's exhortation that we make our forbearance known to all men. Because the Lord is near, we have no excuse for not making known our forbearance. Often we fail to exercise forbearance because we forget that the Lord is near. We do not even remember that He is actually within us. When a brother's wife serves him a cold drink instead of a hot one, will he care for the drink or for the Lord? If he cares about the drink instead of the Lord, then in his experience only the drink will be at hand, for the Lord will be far away. Because we do not realize that the Lord is near, we do not exercise forbearance.

Instead, we are strict in dealing with others and make exacting demands of them without considering their situation. The more we realize the nearness of the Lord, the more satisfied we shall be and the more we shall be considerate of others and sweetly reasonable regarding their situation. If we realize that the Lord is near, we shall turn from the old creation to the new creation, to the out-resurrection, which is expressed as forbearance.

THE EXPRESSION OF THE OUT-RESURRECTION

For Jesus, the Nazarene, to live a life full of forbearance required that He live a life in resurrection. Only a life in the out-resurrection can be a life of forbearance. Forbearance is actually the expression of a living which is in the out-resurrection, in the new creation instead of the old creation. To let our forbearance be known to all men is not simply to be kind or patient. Rather, it is to let others see a proper Christian living. This living is Christ as the out-resurrection expressed through forbearance.

CONSIDERING OTHERS

We have emphasized the need of forbearance in the church life and in our family life. If we are forbearing, we shall be considerate in dealing with others. For example, suppose one sister wants to help another sister improve her way of serving in the church. The sister who wants to offer help needs to consider whether or not the sister she intends to help is able to receive correction. She should also consider whether in offering correction she herself is in the spirit or in the flesh.

Forbearance requires that we not speak to others in haste. On the contrary, we need to have much consideration before saying anything. We can damage brothers and sisters in the church and also members of our family by being too hasty in dealing with them.

I can testify that, as an elderly man, I now deal with my family in a way much different from the way I practiced forty years ago. Today I show much more forbearance than I did then. Previously I stood on my position as a husband and father and said whatever I felt was necessary. However, I learned that this practice was often harmful to others. Now before saying certain things to my wife, I consider her and her situation. I ask myself if she is able to bear what I intend to say and when is the right time to say it. I also consider how happy and comforted she is and how much she is able to receive what I desire to say to her. All this is involved in showing forbearance.

When the Lord Jesus walked with the two disciples on the way to Emmaus, He displayed forbearance. When He asked them what they were talking about, one of them replied, "Art thou only a stranger in Jerusalem, and hast not known the things which are come to pass there in these days?" (Luke 24:18). Even though He knew all things, the Lord asked them, "What things?" (v. 18). Then He patiently listened to them while they told Him what had happened. Later, at the appropriate time, the Lord made Himself known to them. He certainly was forbearing with those disciples.

If we show forbearance toward others, they will be nourished, healed, and helped to grow. We shall not cause them to stumble or hurt them in any way. However, because of our lack of forbearance, we have damaged others in the church and in our family life.

LIVING IN THE OUT-RESURRECTION

I wish to emphasize the fact that forbearance is not a matter of ethics. Forbearance is Christ. In chapters one, two, and three of Philippians, Paul has much to say concerning Christ. Then in 4:5 he speaks of forbearance, not of Christ. Actually, when he says, "Let your forbearance be known to all men," he is saying, "Let Christ be manifested and magnified before all men." After speaking about living Christ, magnifying Christ, taking Christ as the pattern, and pursuing Christ as the goal, Paul indicates that we need to live this Christ as our forbearance. We all need the Lord to be our forbearance. To live Him as forbearance is truly to live in the out-resurrection.

Chapter Two

A LIFE FULL OF FORBEARANCE BUT WITHOUT ANXIETY

(2)

Scripture Reading: Phil. 4:1, 4-5, 11-13; 1 Tim. 3:3;
Titus 3:2; James 3:17

In Philippians 4:5 Paul says, "Let your forbearance be known to all men." Although we are familiar with the word *forbearance,* it is not easy for us to define it adequately. Many would say that forbearance is patience. However, this term is used at the end of a book which emphasizes the experience of Christ. Philippians is not primarily concerned with morality, behavior, character, or ethics. The subject of this Epistle is the experience of Christ. All four chapters of this book are related to the experience of Christ.

MAKING CHRIST KNOWN

As we read the first several verses of chapter four, we may not have the impression that these verses still have the experience of Christ as their subject. But verse 13 says, "I can do all things in Him who empowers me." "All things" must include the exercise of forbearance spoken of in verse 5. Paul charged the saints to have forbearance. Certainly he himself lived a life of forbearance. Otherwise, he would have been hypocritical in exhorting others to make their forbearance known when he himself did not practice forbearance. Paul's word in 4:5 must be based on his own living, experience, and practice. Thus, forbearance must be an experience of Christ. Furthermore, the fact that Paul says that he can do all things in Him who empowers him is an indication that forbearance is Christ.

In 1:20 and 21 Paul speaks of magnifying Christ and of living Him. In chapter two he presents Christ as our unique pattern and then speaks of holding forth the word of life. Holding forth the word of life is equal to expressing Christ. In chapter three we see that Christ should be our goal and prize. We need to pursue toward the goal for the high calling of God in Christ Jesus (3:14). Whether we are young or old, we all should pursue Christ. This was Paul's concept when he said in 3:16, "Only this, whereunto we have attained, by the same rule let us walk." We all should live Christ, magnify Christ, express Christ, and pursue Christ. Then in chapter four Paul speaks of standing firm in the Lord, rejoicing in Him, and letting our forbearance be known to all men. If we have a proper understanding of the subject of Philippians, realizing that this book is focused on the experience of Christ, we shall see that to make our forbearance known is actually to make Christ known. I believe that this was Paul's thought.

The best way to understand the Bible is to get into the thought of the writer and grasp the major points according to which he wrote a particular book. No doubt, by considering the four chapters of Philippians, we shall see that Paul's basic thought in this Epistle is that Christ was his living, pattern, goal with the prize, and power. In this book Paul is saying that we need to live Christ, take Christ as our pattern, pursue Christ as our goal, and experience Christ as our power. All this should result in a certain kind of living, a living which expresses Christ.

AN EXPRESSION OF CHRIST

What word would you use to describe a life that expresses Christ? Would you describe it as loving, submissive, patient, humble, kind? None of these words is adequate. Yes, a life that expresses Christ certainly is loving, submissive, patient, humble, and kind; however, it includes much more than this. It is significant that Paul does not use any of these terms in 4:5. Instead, he uses the word *forbearance*. He does not tell us to make our love or patience known, but to make our forbearance known.

In 4:5 why does Paul tell us to make our forbearance known to all men? Why does he not speak of some other virtue, such as holiness or righteousness? What word would you have used if you were writing this Epistle? Perhaps some would use *faithfulness, obedience,* or *oneness.* But none of these words seems to fit. It does not seem adequate to say, "Let your faithfulness be made known," or, "Let your oneness be made known." Try as we may, we cannot find an adequate replacement for the word *forbearance.* Even though we cannot fully define forbearance or explain what it is, we sense as we read this verse that forbearance is the only word which is fitting in this verse.

When Paul says that we should make our forbearance known to all men, he indicates the fullness of our forbearance. A forbearance which can be made known to all is not a limited or partial forbearance; it is the fullness of forbearance.

If we would understand the meaning of forbearance, we should not turn to books of philosophy or ethics. Instead, we need to turn to the Bible and seek to learn from the Scriptures the significance of forbearance in 4:5. As we have seen, this must be an expression of Christ. First Paul charges us to make our forbearance known to all men. Realizing that we are not able to do this, he goes on to say, "I can do all things in the One who empowers me." This indicates that forbearance is at least part of the expression of Christ.

That forbearance is related to the expression of Christ becomes even more clear when we consider 4:5 in the context of the whole book of Philippians. In 1:20 and 21 Paul speaks of magnifying Christ and living Him. Certainly making our forbearance known must involve living Christ and magnifying Him. This means that our forbearance must be the very Christ we live and magnify. We should not separate chapter four from the rest of the book. In chapter one Paul speaks of magnifying Christ and then, toward the end of the book, of making our forbearance known. The forbearance we make known must be the very Christ we magnify.

In chapter two Paul presents Christ as our unique pattern. Certainly, forbearance must be related to Christ as our pattern. This means that forbearance must involve the experience and the expression of Christ as the pattern revealed in chapter two.

As we have pointed out, in chapter three we have Christ as our goal. With Paul, we must pursue toward this goal. Christ as the goal toward which we pursue must include forbearance. Otherwise, how could Paul encourage us to pursue Christ in chapter three and then in 4:5 charge us to make something other than Christ known to all men? That would not be logical. For Paul to be consistent, what he charges us to make known in 4:5 must be the very goal toward which he encourages us to pursue in chapter three. Since Paul encourages us to pursue Christ, in 4:5 he must not be telling us to make something other than Christ known to all men. Since Paul speaks so much of Christ in the first three chapters of the book, what he says in chapter four must also be related to Christ. Therefore, we believe that the forbearance in 4:5 is Christ.

If the word *forbearance* in 4:5 can be replaced by any other word, it must be the word *Christ*. Instead of saying, "Let your forbearance be made known," we can say, "Let your Christ be made known." This means to let the Christ whom we live and magnify, whom we take as our pattern and pursue as our goal, be made known to all men.

MAKING OUR FORBEARANCE KNOWN

Forbearance is Christ as our living. The Christ whom we live becomes the forbearance we exercise and make known. If we see this, we shall realize that forbearance is a matter of great significance. It is by no means an isolated virtue in the Christian life. On the contrary, forbearance is actually a synonym for Christ in our Christian living. On the one hand, we may say that our Christian life is Christ. On the other hand, we may say that the Christian life is a life of forbearance. To make our forbearance known, therefore, means to make our Christ known.

If we do not make known our forbearance, we shall have Christ only in doctrine or terminology, but we shall not have Christ in our experience. Young people, your parents may know that Christ is in you. However, you need to let Christ be made known to your parents by making your forbearance known to them. To all those whom we contact day by day we need to let our Christ be made known. This is to let our forbearance be known to all men.

I wish to emphasize the fact that forbearance is nothing less than Christ Himself. In doctrine, we may talk about Christ; but in our experience, we need to have forbearance. To let our forbearance be made known is to make known to others the Christ whom we experience, live, and magnify. This is the proper understanding of 4:5 in the light of Christian experience.

In every chapter of Philippians Christ is revealed. However, in chapter four a particular term—forbearance—is used to denote Christ in our experience. Do not think that chapter four of Philippians is on a lower level than chapters one, two, and three. No, in chapter four we have Christ experienced by us and expressed through us as forbearance. We may say that the central focus of our Christian life is Christ. I certainly agree with such a statement. But from the standpoint of our practical Christian experience, the focus of the Christian life is forbearance. Forbearance is an all-inclusive Christian virtue. It includes love, patience, kindness, humility, compassion, considerateness, and submissiveness, a willingness to yield. If we have such an all-inclusive virtue, we shall also have righteousness and holiness.

The Christian life is a life full of forbearance but without anxiety. Only when we have forbearance can we have a life without anxiety. If our whole being is filled with forbearance, there will not be any room for anxiety.

FITTING AND SUITABLE

The Greek word for *forbearance* is rendered different ways by different translations. Some versions translate the Greek word as *yieldingness*. The word used in the Chinese version means to give in humbly. These understandings are correct, but they are rather shallow. Other translators point out that the Greek word means "reasonable, considerate, suitable, and fitting." A forbearing person is one who always fits in, one whose behavior is always suitable.

Certain saints are good, but they do not fit in. They may move from place to place, but no matter where they may go, they are not happy. The reason these saints do not fit in is that they are not forbearing. A forbearing person is one who always fits in, whose behavior is always suitable, no matter what the circumstances or environment may be.

Forbearance also includes peacefulness, mildness, and gentleness. If you are reasonable, considerate, and able to fit in, you will no doubt be gentle, kind, mild, and peaceful. You will also be meek and moderate, full of compassion for others. As we pointed out in the previous chapter, the opposite of forbearance is being just in a very exacting way. A person who lacks forbearance will be exacting and demanding of others. But to be forbearing means that we are satisfied with less than our due. Alford says that the Greek word for *forbearance* means to not be strict with respect to legal rights. For example, a certain thing may be ours, but we do not claim it according to strict, legal right. This is forbearance.

THE FORBEARANCE OF CHRIST

The life of the Lord Jesus is the best illustration of forbearance. Consider how He spoke to those two disciples on the way to Emmaus. Luke 24:15 says that while these disciples "communed together and reasoned, Jesus himself drew near, and went with them." The Lord Jesus said to them, "What manner of communications are these that ye have one to another, as ye walk, and are sad?" (v. 17). With a rebuking tone, one of the disciples answered, "Art thou only a stranger in Jerusalem, and hast not known the things which are come to pass there in these days?" (v. 18). Appearing not to know anything, the Lord asked, "What things?" (v. 19). Then they proceeded to tell Him about Jesus of Nazareth, One they described as a "prophet mighty in deed and word before God and all the people." They went on to say that the chief priests and the rulers delivered Him to be condemned to death and crucified Him. How forbearing the Lord was to listen to the disciples speak things which He knew much better than they did! After walking quite a distance, "they drew nigh unto the village, whither they went: and he made as though he would have gone further" (v. 28). However, "they constrained him, saying, Abide with us; for it is toward evening, and the day is far spent. And he went in to tarry with them." (v. 29). The Lord even sat down to dine with them. When He took bread, blessed it, broke it, and gave it to them, "their eyes were opened, and they knew him" (v. 31). In all this we see the Lord's forbearance.

Besides the Lord Jesus, no human being has ever practiced a life of such forbearance. If you study the biographies of famous people, you will see that not one was truly a person of forbearance. However, if you read the four Gospels, you will see that the human living of the Lord Jesus was full of forbearance. The Lord Jesus exercised forbearance with His disciples. Can you find a case where the Lord Jesus "fired" one of them? The Lord was forbearing even with Judas.

CHRIST AS OUR FORBEARANCE

We need forbearance in the church life, especially in our serving together. Suppose a particular sister is serving in a way that is not adequate. The sister serving with her faces at least four options: walk away, join her in serving in her poor way, correct her, or try to improve her. None of these options involves forbearance. If the one sister exercises forbearance, she certainly will not walk away from the other sister. At least for a while, she will join the sister in her serving. Then she will exercise wisdom to see the sister's situation and to determine whether or not she can speak a word of correction or improvement in love. If the sister is not able to receive such a word, the other one needs to wait before saying anything. Eventually, she may have an opportunity to speak not according to her own intention, but according to the leading of the Spirit. This is to exercise forbearance. If we all exercise forbearance, the church will be built up in a wonderful way.

The virtue of forbearance is all-inclusive. It includes love, kindness, mercy, reasonableness, the ability to fit in, and many other virtues. Perhaps now we can understand why Paul speaks of forbearance toward the end of a profound book on the experience of Christ. When Paul exhorts us to let our forbearance be made known to all men, he is saying something of great significance. No human being is able by the natural life to fulfill such a requirement. Confucius may have been very good, but he was still sinful and fallen. Only the Lord Jesus lived a life full of forbearance, and only Christ can be our perfect forbearance today. The best word to sum up the totality of Christ's human virtues is *forbearance*. To make known our forbearance is to live a life which expresses Christ; it is to express the Christ by whom we live. Such a life is Christ Himself as the totality of all human virtues. This is Christ as our forbearance.

A LIFE FULL OF FORBEARANCE
BUT WITHOUT ANXIETY

(3)

Scripture Reading: Phil. 4:1-2, 4-7, 11-13; 3:15-16

The Greek word for "forbearance" is composed of two words. The first is the preposition *epi* which, when added to another word, can have the meaning of extensive or full. This word is a component of the Greek word for "full knowledge" used in 2 Timothy 2:25. The second Greek word has various meanings: "reasonable, considerate, and suitable." Thus, the meaning of the Greek is "extensively reasonable or fully reasonable."

AN ALL-INCLUSIVE VIRTUE

Based on the analysis of the Greek word, our spiritual experience, God's activities in His economy, and the Lord's living on earth, we can realize that to have adequate forbearance requires that we also have many other virtues. Forbearance is an all-inclusive virtue.

Of the many human virtues, Paul chose to speak of forbearance in Philippians 4:5. As we shall see, this particular virtue is related to other important matters in Philippians 3 and 4. For example, it is related to being able to do all things in Christ and also to learning the secret of contentment in all circumstances. Furthermore, in order to have forbearance we must be qualified according to what is mentioned in 3:15 and 16.

Forbearance means to be fully reasonable, considerate, and suitable. This requires a genuine understanding of the situation at hand. Suppose two students are arguing about a problem in mathematics. Unable to settle their argument, they bring the problem to you. But if you are ignorant of mathematics, it will not be possible for you to give them a fair and reasonable judgment. Even if you have the necessary understanding, you may lack wisdom to deal with the people involved.

THE NEED OF FORBEARANCE
IN OUR FAMILY LIFE

There is a great need of forbearance in our family life. A good family life is the product of forbearance. If a husband and wife show forbearance toward each other and toward their children, they will have an excellent married life and family life. However, if they do not exercise forbearance, they will seriously damage their life together as a family.

In dealing with their children, parents should be neither too strict nor too tolerant. Both excessive strictness and excessive tolerance are damaging to children. Then what is the right way for parents to care for their children? The right way is the way which is full of forbearance.

Suppose a child does something wrong, and the matter is made known to his father. He should not rebuke his child in a hasty way or spank him in anger. In Ephesians 6 Paul tells us not to provoke our children. Usually parents provoke their children by dealing with them in anger. If you are angry with your child, you first need to ask the Lord to take away your anger. Once your anger has been dealt with by the Lord, you need to exercise your understanding to realize why the child made that particular mistake. No doubt, the child was wrong. Nevertheless, you still must understand his situation. Perhaps he was wrong because you were careless. If you had not been careless in that particular way, the child would not have made that mistake. Because your carelessness afforded him the opportunity to do something wrong, you should not put the full blame on him. Rather, first you must blame yourself and then discipline the child. All this is included in exercising forbearance toward our children.

Parents need to exercise wisdom in speaking to their children. A child may need correction, but the parents need to sense when is the right time to speak to him. A father should

ask himself whether or not he should rebuke his child in front
of other children or even in front of the mother. Sometimes it
is not wise to discipline a child in the presence of others. How
much wisdom we must exercise in caring for our children! If
we do not have forbearance, we shall not exercise wisdom. On
the other hand, if we do not have adequate wisdom, we shall
not be able to exercise forbearance.

If we would show forbearance, we also need patience. Most
parents find it difficult to be patient when they are disciplin-
ing their children. Suppose a brother is about to rebuke one of
his children. It would be much better if he waited a few hours
before saying anything. However, it is extremely difficult to
wait even a few minutes, much less a few hours. The natural
tendency is to deal with the children in haste. Such impatience is damaging.

Impatience is also damaging in our married life. Suppose
a brother feels it is necessary to speak to his wife about a certain matter that is not pleasant. If he is truly forbearing, he
will wait for the right time to speak, a time when the conversation will be constructive. In the same principle, a wife needs
to be patient with her husband and wait for the proper time
to express her feelings about certain matters. However, to be
patient and forbearing in such a way is very difficult for us.

As an all-inclusive virtue, forbearance implies not only
understanding, wisdom, and patience, but also mercy, kindness, love, and sympathy. The list of virtues is almost endless.
As we have pointed out, the Greek word rendered *forbearance*
implies considerateness. To be forbearing is to consider the
situation of others. If we would exercise forbearance in our
married life and family life, we would have a pleasant married life and an excellent family life.

NEEDED BY ELDERS

In 1 Timothy 3:3 Paul indicates that the elders in a local
church need to be forbearing. If the elders do not have adequate
forbearance, the church in their locality will not be built up.

We know from Ephesians 4 and Colossians 3 that the church
is the new man, made up of believers with different nationali-
ties and cultures. A great deal of forbearance is needed to

build up a church composed of saints with many different backgrounds. The elders need a proper understanding of all the saints and their particular characters. They also need to exercise wisdom in caring for them. If the elders lack understanding and wisdom, they will not be able to exercise forbearance and may cause a great deal of damage. For the building up among the saints in a local church, the virtue most needed by every elder is forbearance.

NEEDED BY ALL THE SAINTS

In the church forbearance is needed not only by the elders, but also by all the saints. We especially need to exercise forbearance when we come together in different groups for the church service. As we serve together in the church, we need to show forbearance toward one another. On the one hand, we should not reject anyone; on the other hand, we should not be excessively tolerant with someone who serves in a way that is not adequate. How we need forbearance!

GOD'S FORBEARANCE

The Bible reveals that in His economy God has exercised great forbearance. Immediately after the fall of man, God began to show forbearance in His dealings with man. If you read Genesis 3 from the viewpoint of forbearance, you will see how forbearing God was with fallen man. God exercised His understanding, fully realizing man's situation and need. He also exercised His wisdom to deal with fallen man.

For the accomplishment of His eternal purpose, for the carrying out of His economy, God has always exercised forbearance. With His forbearance, He has understanding, wisdom, mercy, kindness, love, and grace. Even the rich supply of life is included in God's forbearance. God never commands us to do anything without considering our need and granting us His supply. If a parent charges his children to do a certain task but does not supply them with what they need, that parent is not forbearing. Forbearance always includes the adequate supply to meet the need.

As we read the Bible, we see that God dealt with different people in different ways. For example, He dealt with Adam in one way, with Abel in another way, and with Cain in yet another way. Some students of the Bible say that in the Scriptures there are different dispensations, different ways God deals with man. These dispensations are actually related to forbearance. For God to deal with people in a particular way during a certain age is for Him to show forbearance. Because God is forbearing, He knows how to deal with everyone. He may come to you in a certain way because He knows that you are a certain kind of person. However, He may approach another person in a very different way.

The Bible reveals that God exercises forbearance in carrying out His economy. If God had dealt with fallen man in the way we deal with others, there would have been no way for Him to fulfill His purpose. But God has made His forbearance known to all men. Thus, God Himself set up an example, a pattern, of forbearance, making known His forbearance to men throughout all generations. God makes known His forbearance by dealing with us in a way that is reasonable, suitable, and considerate. God never disciplines anyone without proper consideration. He often waits a long period of time before chastising someone. God certainly is forbearing and full of understanding, wisdom, patience, consideration, sympathy, mercy, kindness, love, and the supply of life. Consider, for example, how forbearing He was in dealing with Israel. If you read of Israel's journey in the wilderness, you will see that God truly was forbearing toward them. God has also been forbearing with us. He has dealt with us like a wise and loving father, full of forbearance.

A BOOK OF FORBEARANCE

The entire Bible reveals the divine forbearance. We may even say that the Bible is a book of forbearance and that, as revealed in the Scriptures, God Himself is forbearance. Hence, if you ask me to define forbearance, I would say firstly that forbearance is God.

CHRIST'S FORBEARANCE

As we have pointed out in foregoing chapters, Christ Himself is our forbearance. The four Gospels reveal that the Lord

Jesus lived a life of forbearance. He was forbearing with Judas and in His dealings with Peter. When He was twelve years old, He exercised forbearance toward His mother, Mary, and Joseph. In case after case, the Lord displayed understanding, wisdom, patience, mercy, kindness, and love. He was kind toward Judas, and with Peter He was full of grace.

An excellent example of Christ's forbearance toward Peter is found in Matthew 17:24 and 25. Those who received the half-shekel for the poll tax came to Peter and asked, "Does not your teacher pay the half-shekel?" (v. 24). Immediately Peter answered, "Yes." When he came into the house, the Lord Jesus did not rebuke him. Rather, He spoke to him in a way that was full of forbearance. Eventually, the Lord Jesus even gave Peter a means of supply to pay the poll tax. By exercising forbearance toward Peter the Lord Jesus also taught him forbearance. No doubt, when Peter was waiting for a fish with a shekel in its mouth, he had a good opportunity to be forbearing.

In John 11 we see the Lord's forbearance with Martha and Mary, the sisters of Lazarus. Instead of acting in haste when He heard that Lazarus was sick, the Lord deliberately delayed. Through this delay others were exposed. In dealing with this situation the Lord exercised much understanding, wisdom, consideration, mercy, and kindness. Eventually there was a great supply of life manifested in the resurrection of Lazarus.

PAUL'S FORBEARANCE

Paul's life was also a testimony of forbearance. He wrote the book of Philippians from a prison in Rome. Paul was suffering, and according to chapter four, he was short of supply and in want. Among all the churches, the church in Philippi was the best in caring for Paul's needs. But for some reason, according to the Lord's sovereignty, there was a period of time when the Philippians seemingly forgot Paul and his need. This was the reason he says in 4:10, "But I rejoiced in the Lord greatly that now at length you caused your thinking for me to blossom anew." This word implies that Paul had passed through a "winter" of suffering and that "spring" had come with the blossoming anew of the Philippians' concern for him.

But even though Paul was suffering imprisonment, perse-
cution, attack, negligence, and the lack of supply, he still
exercised forbearance and could declare, "I have learned, in
whatever circumstances I am, to be content. I know both how
to be abased, and I know how to abound; in everything and in
all things I have learned the secret both to be filled and to
hunger, both to abound and to be in want. I can do all things
in Him who empowers me" (4:11-13). Before he charged the
saints to let their forbearance be known to all men, he exercised forbearance himself. No doubt, Paul's forbearance was
made known to those around him. He was full of understanding, wisdom, considerateness, sympathy, mercy, and kindness.
He was also full of the life supply.

If we read the book of Philippians carefully, we shall see
that 3:17-21 is a separate section. This means that, spiritu-
ally speaking, 4:1 is the continuation of 3:16. After exhorting
the saints to walk by the same rule, Paul charges them to
"stand firm in the Lord" (4:1). Then he urges them to rejoice
in the Lord (v. 4) and to let their forbearance be known to all
men (v. 5). Later in chapter four he testifies that he can do all
things in the One who empowers him. Thus, Paul could make
his forbearance known to the saints because he was in the
One who empowered him. Furthermore, he was content,
having learned the secret both how to be abased and how to
abound.

THE NEED OF GROWTH

It is not easy to make our forbearance known to all men.
This requires growth, in both our human life and our spiritual life. The more a person grows and matures, the more forbearance he has. Therefore, forbearance requires the growth
of life. It demands maturity.

In 3:15 Paul says, "Let us therefore, as many as are
full-grown, have this mind." We have pointed out that to have
this mind is to have the mind to live Christ and pursue Him.
However, the very Christ whom we live and pursue should be
expressed as forbearance. If we put together these verses
from chapters three and four, we see that forbearance requires

maturity. Without growth and maturity it will be extremely difficult to make known our forbearance.

We should not expect a new believer in Christ to be able to exercise much forbearance. Instead of requiring a new believer to exercise forbearance, we should be the ones to be forbearing. For example, in a family the parents must first be forbearing and thereby set up an example of forbearance for the children to follow. If a brother is not forbearing toward his wife and children, he should not expect his children to know what forbearance is. Instead of commanding others to be forbearing, he himself should establish a pattern of forbearance for his children to follow. As we have indicated, to have such forbearance requires maturity.

WALKING BY THE RULE OF FORBEARANCE

In 3:16 Paul says, "Only this, whereunto we have attained, by the same rule let us walk." It is true that the rule here is the rule of pursuing Christ. But since in our practical daily life Christ is to be expressed as forbearance, we may say that to walk by the same rule is to walk by the rule of forbearance.

THE SECRET OF CONTENTMENT

After speaking of forbearance in 4:5, Paul says, "I have learned, in whatever circumstances I am, to be content" (v. 11). Paul had learned the secret of contentment. By this we see that in order to be forbearing, we must be satisfied and content. If we are not content, we shall not be able to forbear.

From experience I can testify that whenever I am not satisfied, I am not able to exercise forbearance. But whenever I am satisfied and content, it is easy to be forbearing.

When a person is happy, he is not easily upset. But if he is unhappy, tired, hungry, and thirsty, he can be upset easily. A satisfied person, on the contrary, is pleasant and happy. When we are full of joy, it is difficult for us to become angry. Those who are parents know that if a child misbehaves when we are satisfied and happy, we shall deal with the child in one way, in a way full of forbearance. But if he behaves in exactly the same way when we are dissatisfied and unhappy, we shall deal with him differently, in a way that is short of forbearance. The difference is that on one occasion we are full of Christ and are happy and satisfied, whereas on the other occasion we are short of Christ and short of satisfaction in Him.

Paul could let his forbearance be known to all the saints because he was content. He did not lack anything but was fully satisfied. No matter how he was treated by others, no matter whether the saints in Philippi cared for his need or not, Paul was satisfied. His life was full of contentment.

Now we can see that forbearance requires maturity of life and also satisfaction and contentment in Christ. Few of us are fully mature, but we can thank the Lord that we are mature at least to some extent. According to our degree of maturity, we enjoy the contentment of the Lord's life. Knowing contentment and satisfaction, we can then exercise our forbearance.

The more the elders in a church become mature and content, the easier it will be for them to exercise forbearance in the house of God. In like manner, the more a father is mature and content, the easier it will be for him to exercise forbearance with the members of his family. No doubt, as the ancient One, our God is mature, satisfied, and content to the uttermost. Thus, He is able to exercise His forbearance in full. The Lord Jesus also had the growth in life, the satisfaction of life, and the contentment of life. Therefore, wherever He was, He was full of forbearance and could exercise His forbearance toward all.

When we live such a life full of forbearance, we shall not have any anxiety. In the following chapters we shall see that when our living is full of forbearance, we shall be free from anxiety.

A LIFE FULL OF FORBEARANCE
BUT WITHOUT ANXIETY

(4)

Scripture Reading: Phil. 4:4-7, 10-13

In the foregoing chapter we emphasized the need of forbearance in our married life, family life, and church life. For the building up of the church, the elders and all the saints need to exercise forbearance. Likewise, for a pleasant married life and an excellent family life we need to be forbearing. I hope that all the saints with children will be deeply impressed with the need to exercise forbearance in their daily living at home.

THE MEANING OF FORBEARANCE

The Greek word rendered *forbearance* in Philippians 4:5 is composed of two words: *epi,* a preposition which means unto, and *eikos,* which means seemly, fitting, or suitable. When the preposition *epi* is added to other Greek words as a prefix, it often bears the meaning of full or extensive. Consider, for example, the word *epignosis* used in 2 Timothy 2:25. In this verse Paul speaks of "the full knowledge of the truth." Hence, *epi* added to *gnosis* gives a word which means full knowledge. The use of this preposition as a component of the Greek word for "forbearance" in 4:5 indicates that the meaning of this word is to be fully reasonable, or fitting or suitable to the fullest extent. We need to have a full and extensive reasonableness and considerateness. Furthermore, we need to act in a way that is fitting and suitable to the fullest extent. All these meanings are included in the Greek word used by Paul in 4:5.

The Greek word rendered *forbearance* in 4:5 is not actually a noun; it is an adjective used as a noun with a definite article. This use of an adjective as a noun serves to emphasize the meaning of the word. For example, in 1 Timothy 6:17 Paul says, "Charge those who are rich in the present age not to be high-minded." This is more emphatic than saying, "Charge the rich man not to be high-minded." In Philippians 4:5 Paul deliberately uses an adjective as a noun in order to place special emphasis on forbearance.

A RICH SUPPLY

In the previous chapter we pointed out that forbearance requires understanding, wisdom, patience, and many other virtues. If we would be forbearing, we need to be merciful, kind, and compassionate. Furthermore, to forbear definitely requires a certain ability in a number of areas. We need the ability to understand, to be patient, to help others, and to afford them the necessary supply. In His forbearance toward us, God certainly has given us a rich supply.

God forbears with fallen man for a purpose. His purpose in showing forbearance is to accomplish His economy. If God did not afford man the adequate supply and show forbearance to man, there would be no way for God to fulfill His purpose of accomplishing His economy.

REJOICING IN THE LORD

We have seen that forbearance requires maturity and also satisfaction and contentment. Now we need to see that forbearance is also related to rejoicing in the Lord. In 4:4 Paul says, "Rejoice in the Lord always; again I will say, rejoice." Immediately after this he says, "Let your forbearance be known to all men." If we do not rejoice in the Lord, we shall not be able to forbear. If we would make known our forbearance, we need to be happy and joyful in the Lord. Those who are sad or sorrowful cannot have forbearance. Instead, they find it easy to be upset, to complain, or to lose their temper. Forbearance in 4:5 is the issue, the result, of rejoicing in the Lord, mentioned in verse 4. From experience we know that rejoicing and forbearing go together.

A PATTERN OF FORBEARANCE

In 4:11-13 we see the relationship between contentment and forbearance. In verse 11 Paul testifies, "I have learned, in whatever circumstances I am, to be content." In verse 12 he goes on to say, "I know both how to be abased, and I know how to abound; in everything and in all things I have learned the secret both to be filled and to hunger, both to abound and to be in want." Because Paul had learned the secret of contentment, he was able to forbear with all the churches and all the saints. He says, "I can do all things in Him who empowers me" (v. 13). According to the context, this includes the ability to make His forbearance known to the saints.

Consider Paul's situation when he wrote the book of Philippians. His circumstances were not at all positive. He was a prisoner in Rome; he was opposed by the religionists; and even the saints, including the Philippians who had been faithful to supply his needs in the past, neglected him for a period of time. In 4:10 Paul says, "But I rejoiced in the Lord greatly that now at length you caused your thinking for me to blossom anew; wherein you did indeed take thought, but you lacked opportunity." The words *blossom anew* imply that Paul had passed through a "winter" in his experience, but now it was "spring," with the Philippians' concern for him blossoming anew. Although Paul alluded to his "winter" experience and the saints' temporary neglect of him, he exercised great understanding in writing to them. As he was composing this Epistle, he exercised forbearance. Thus, the apostle Paul, one who was full of understanding concerning the situation and concerning the saints, was an excellent pattern of forbearance.

THE NEED FOR UNDERSTANDING AND WISDOM

Often we are not forbearing because of misunderstanding. In the church life often we may not understand the brothers and sisters. In our family life we may fail to understand our husband or wife. This lack of understanding causes a lack of forbearance. Suppose Paul had misunderstood the Philippians. He certainly would not have written them such a marvelous

Epistle. Instead, he might have pointed out that when he most needed their help, it was not forthcoming. Now that they remembered him and sent him a gift, it arrived too late. Paul, however, had a full understanding of God's economy and His move; he also understood the subtlety of Satan's attack. Moreover, he understood the saints in Philippi and their situation. To him everything was crystal clear. Thus, on his part there was no misunderstanding. He could exercise much forbearance in writing to the believers in Philippi.

In writing to the Philippians, Paul also exercised wisdom. He knew what to say and how much to say. If we read this Epistle carefully, we shall realize that Paul's wording is very exact. Paul wrote in a way that was neither too lengthy nor too brief. Here we see Paul's wisdom.

Paul needed to exercise wisdom in writing to the Philippians, and there is the need for us also to exercise wisdom in our married life. Husbands need wisdom in speaking with their wives, and wives need wisdom in sharing matters with their husbands. Here I would emphasize the need for the wife to have wisdom toward her husband. Suppose a sister intends to talk about a particular matter with her husband. Before she says anything, she needs to exercise understanding, consideration, and wisdom. If she speaks to him at the wrong time or if she says too much to him concerning the subject at hand, she may cause him to become angry not only with her but also with others in the church life, even with the elders. Sometimes a husband becomes upset with the elders simply because his wife gives him information without exercising understanding, consideration, and wisdom. Even in passing on information to her husband, a sister needs a great deal of forbearance. For this, she needs a proper understanding of her husband and of his situation. If she realizes that her husband is a quick person, one who reacts hastily to things and who is easily angered or upset, she needs to consider how to help him to be patient and slow down. In particular, she needs to consider how much she should speak to him. Perhaps at first she should share only part of the information. Before saying more, she should consider the atmosphere and discern whether it is the proper time for her husband to hear more.

She may share something at one time, something further at another time, and the remainder at still another time. If the sister is forbearing, exercising understanding, consideration, and wisdom, the result of her speaking with her husband will be very profitable both for their married life and for the church life.

PRAYER AND FORBEARANCE

Just as verse 5 is the continuation of verse 4, so verse 6 is the continuation of verse 5. If we see the continuation here, we shall realize that forbearance requires prayer. In verse 6 Paul says, "In nothing be anxious, but in everything, by prayer and petition with thanksgiving, let your requests be made known to God." There does not seem to be a relation between the words "let your forbearance be known" and "let your requests be made known." Actually, they are closely related. When we exercise forbearance, we shall realize how much we need to pray. We may be anxious and fearful about many things concerning our family or concerning the church. Furthermore, we may realize that if we talk about our concerns, we may cause problems. What then should we do? After charging us not to be anxious, Paul urges us to pray. If we pray, the Lord will give us the understanding, consideration, and wisdom we need. If a sister prays before sharing a particular matter with her husband, she will know what to say to him and when is the proper time to speak. Furthermore, if she is faithful to pray, she will also have a rich supply to minister to her husband. Then her forbearance with its rich supply will accomplish God's purpose in that situation.

If all the saints in the Lord's recovery exercise forbearance in their married life and also in training their children, we shall have the best family life. Then we shall be able to sing about the wonderful, glorious church life. We shall be able to testify not only of a wonderful church life, but also of a wonderful married life.

MARRIED LIFE, FAMILY LIFE, AND THE CHURCH LIFE

First we need to build up the proper married life and family life, and then we shall be able to build up the church life. If a brother does not know how to build up a pleasant married life at home and an excellent family life with his children, it will be very difficult for him to share in building up the church. When he comes together with others for the church service, he may exercise politeness. However, he may not be polite to his wife or children. We may be polite to the brothers and sisters in the church but be very impolite to our husband or wife or to our children.

Our home life is where we are exposed the most. Do not think that simply because a certain brother is nice, kind, and polite with the saints in the church he is necessarily that way at home. If you want to know him, you need to see how he lives with his wife and children. Oh, how much we need forbearance in our married life and family life that we may build up the proper church life!

The more we realize the need of forbearance, the more we shall see how difficult it is to be a proper human being. It is not easy to be a wife or husband, a parent, or a member of the church. Most Christians today know nothing of the genuine church life. At most, many gather together for a worship service for an hour on the Lord's Day. There is no practice of the church life. Furthermore, in our society married life has been severely damaged. Many even live together without being married because they do not want to accept the limitations of marriage. This is to utterly forsake the practice of forbearance.

We need to be fully committed to our married life, family life, and the church life. The ties that bind us together are permanent. In the genuine family life and church life, no one is hired or fired. Can we hire someone to be our child, or can we fire one of our children? Of course not. Neither can members of the church be hired or fired. Likewise, if a servant of the Lord can fire one of his co-workers, then they are not truly working together in the Lord. In the Lord's work there is no such thing as hiring or firing. Therefore, in the family life, in the church life, and in working together for the Lord's interests, we need forbearance. Forbearance is necessary because we are bound together permanently.

Once again I would remind you that forbearance is an all-inclusive virtue. This virtue includes understanding, wisdom, patience, consideration, and the ability to help and render the adequate supply. If we all exercise forbearance, we shall have a pleasant married life, an excellent family life, and a wonderful church life.

A LIFE FULL OF FORBEARANCE
BUT WITHOUT ANXIETY

(5)

Scripture Reading: Phil. 4:4-7; 1:18-21; 4:10-13

We have repeatedly emphasized that the book of Philippians is a book on the experience of Christ. To experience Christ we need to live Him that we may magnify Him (1:20-21). Then we need to take Him as our pattern and pursue Him as our goal. In our Christian life we should have the unique mind—the mind to pursue Christ and gain Him. After covering these aspects of the experience of Christ, Paul, somewhat to our surprise, speaks in chapter four of forbearance and anxiety. On the positive side, we need forbearance; on the negative side, we should not have any anxiety.

Why at the conclusion of such a profound book on the experience of Christ does Paul mention forbearance and anxiety? Apparently there is no connection between the matters covered in chapters one, two, and three and Paul's word about forbearance and anxiety. Years ago, I did not consider it worthwhile for Paul to speak of anxiety. According to my concept, he should have continued to speak about higher things, although I was not clear what these higher things should be.

THE CIRCUMSTANCES ASSIGNED BY GOD

In Ephesians 1:3 and 2:6 Paul talks about the heavenlies. In your experience day by day are you in the heavenlies or in anxiety? More often than not, we are in anxiety, not in the heavenlies. After the fall of man, human life became a composition of anxiety and worry. If you read Genesis 3 carefully, you will see that anxiety comes from the environment assigned to us by God. For example, we have anxiety with respect to our children. From the moment a child is born, his parents worry about him. Those who do not have children may dream of having a child one day. But they do not realize the worry and anxiety associated with giving birth to a child and raising him. Everything that affects the living of our children gives rise to anxiety. We may worry about their breathing, their diet, and their clothing. Most parents can testify that as far as their children are concerned, their days are filled more with anxiety than with happiness.

Genesis 3 indicates that fallen man is also anxious about making a living. In Genesis 3:17 the Lord said to the man, "Cursed is the ground for thy sake; in sorrow shalt thou eat of it all the days of thy life." In verse 19 the Lord says, "In the sweat of thy face shalt thou eat bread." Because man must labor to maintain his existence, he is full of anxiety. Every farmer is anxious about his crops. He worries about the weather and also about damage caused by disease and insects. Actually there is not one kind of work which leaves us free from anxiety. Even those who are successful in their profession are anxious about their work. Anxiety is unavoidable.

There is also a good deal of anxiety related to married life. Young people desire to be married. Married life is good, but it involves more worry and anxiety than happiness. I encourage all the young people to get married at the proper time, but they should not expect a married life free from anxiety.

Human life is full of anxiety. Angels, however, are not subject to anxiety because they do not have any circumstances to worry about. They do not marry, and they do not need to be concerned about earning a living or taking care of a family. It is not even necessary for angels to sleep. Some people make the mistake of trying to live as if they were angels. But God has ordained all the circumstances of human life, even though these circumstances give rise more to anxiety than to happiness. It seems that sorrow always lasts longer than happiness. There may be a short period of happiness and then a much longer time of sorrow, worry, or anxiety.

What is God's purpose in assigning circumstances to us

which cause anxiety? According to Romans 8, in addition to redemption and the indwelling Spirit, we need "all things." Verse 28 says, "And we know that God causes all things to work together for good to those who love God, to those who are called according to the purpose." To be sure, included in "all things" are sufferings, anxieties, and worries. In order for God to perfect us, sufferings are necessary. From our experience we know that virtually every matter included in "all things" involves anxiety.

THE TOTALITY OF HUMAN LIFE
AND OF THE CHRISTIAN LIFE

As an elderly person, I have passed through a great many experiences in human life. Under the sovereign hand of the Lord, I have been in a great many different circumstances. I have known poverty, and I have known what it is to have my needs supplied. I can testify that in all the circumstances of human life anxiety is present. *Anxiety* is a word that can sum up human life. The totality of human life is anxiety. If you ask an older person about anxiety, he will tell you that he has known anxiety almost every day of his life.

Paul speaks of anxiety in Philippians 4:6 because he realizes that it is the totality of man's life. Paul also realized that forbearance is the totality of a proper Christian life. Paul knew that human life is constituted of anxiety and that the Christian life is constituted of forbearance. Thus, to live Christ is to have forbearance without anxiety.

It is not possible to understand Philippians 4 adequately simply by studying this chapter in letters. We need experience with the Lord in order to understand Paul's meaning. Fifty years ago I did not have a proper understanding of this chapter. But through many years of study and experience, both in human life and in the Christian life, the Lord has opened my eyes to see that the genuine Christian life is a life of forbearance. I have come to realize that just as anxiety is the totality of human life, so forbearance is the totality of the Christian life. This is the reason Paul uses the words *forbearance* and *anxiety* together in charging the saints. Positively, we should make known our forbearance. All those who come in contact with us should know our forbearance. Negatively, we need to have a life without anxiety.

To be a proper human being we need to be Christians, and to be normal Christians we need to have the church life. However, if we are to have the proper and genuine church life, we need a life full of forbearance but without anxiety. To have such a life is to live Christ.

LIVING CHRIST

In Galatians 2:20 Paul says, "I have been crucified with Christ, and it is no longer I who live, but Christ lives in me." Years ago, I began to read books on this verse. However, I could not understand what it meant for Christ to live in me. The explanation of Galatians 2:20 is found not in Galatians, but in Philippians. In Philippians Paul says not only that Christ lives in us; he goes on to reveal that to live is Christ. To live Christ surpasses simply having Christ live in us. Living Christ means that we have a life full of forbearance but without anxiety.

Any amount of anxiety decreases the measure of Christ in our experience. Even a little anxiety causes the measure of Christ to diminish. The extent to which Christ is present in our daily life is determined by the amount of forbearance and anxiety. If we have forbearance, we have Christ. But if we have anxiety, we are short of Christ. In your living day by day, how much forbearance do you have and how much anxiety? Which is greater—the degree of forbearance or of anxiety? Probably most of us would have to admit that in our daily life we have more anxiety than forbearance.

I wish to emphasize the fact that to live Christ is to have forbearance but no anxiety. If we have forbearance we shall not have anxiety. But if we have anxiety, we shall not have forbearance. Forbearance and anxiety cannot coexist.

MAGNIFYING CHRIST

Philippians 4:4 says, "Rejoice in the Lord always; again I will say, rejoice." Paul opens 4:10 with the words, "But I rejoiced in the Lord greatly." Furthermore, in 1:18 Paul, speaking of his affliction, says, "What then? Only that in every way, whether in pretense or in truth, Christ is announced, and in this I rejoice, yes, and I will rejoice." Paul's word about rejoicing is especially significant when we consider his circumstances. He was a prisoner in Rome, and certain of his opposers were doing everything possible to damage his ministry. Nevertheless, Paul declares, "For I know that for me this shall turn out to salvation through your petition and the bountiful supply of the Spirit of Jesus Christ" (v. 19). As we have pointed out previously, salvation here means to magnify Christ by living Him. Thus, Paul says, "According to my earnest expectation and hope that in nothing I shall be put to shame, but with all boldness, as always, even now Christ shall be magnified in my body, whether through life or through death" (v. 20). Paul did not expect to be put to shame in anything.

Suppose one of Paul's co-workers visited him in prison and found him anxious, sorrowful, and full of worry. No doubt the one visiting him would have said, "What a shame to see the very apostle who ministered Christ to us so sorrowful and anxious!" If this had been Paul's situation, he would have been put to shame. But Paul magnified Christ. No matter how difficult his circumstances were, he did not have any anxiety. Because Paul was not anxious in anything, he was not put to shame in anything. Instead, Christ was magnified in him.

Paul could magnify Christ because he had forbearance. Even during his imprisonment, Paul had a great deal of forbearance. He considered the churches, he had a proper understanding of the saints, and he had the ability to supply the saints and those around him with love, mercy, kindness, and sympathy. Because he exercised his forbearance in full, there was not a trace of anxiety. Paul could even say that he expected Christ to be magnified in him whether through life or through death. This indicates that Paul was not worried about death. The thought of death did not make him anxious.

CONTENTMENT AND FORBEARANCE

We have seen that anxiety is opposed to forbearance. Anxiety is like a worm that devours our ability to forbear. If we have no forbearance, it will be easy for us to be upset or to lose our temper. Anger often comes out of anxiety. If I am worried about my future, my circumstances, or my family, I will not be happy with others. This worry will cause me to be upset with everyone. Only when we are happy and contented do we have forbearance.

In a previous chapter we pointed out that happiness and contentment are two elements which produce forbearance. Only a happy, satisfied person can forbear. One who is sorrowful and discontented, on the contrary, is easily irritated or offended. Because Paul was full of happiness and contentment, with him there was no anxiety but an abundance of forbearance.

We know from Paul's word in 4:10-12 that, at least for a period of time, he was short of supply. But he could testify, "I have learned, in whatever circumstances I am, to be content." He could say, "I know both how to be abased, and I know how to abound; in everything and in all things I have learned the secret both to be filled and to hunger, both to abound and to be in want." Because Paul had learned the secret, he could be content and, as a result, have an abundance of forbearance.

Many have pointed out that Philippians is a book of joy. Again and again Paul exhorts us to rejoice in the Lord. Paul's environment would have made it difficult for anyone to be joyful. We do not usually think of a prison as a place for rejoicing. But because Paul had no anxiety, no worry about his circumstances or future, he could rejoice in the Lord and be forbearing.

GOD'S ASSIGNMENT

If we would have a life free of anxiety, we need to realize that all our circumstances, good or bad, have been assigned to us by God. We need to have this realization with a full assurance. Suppose a brother is in business as a merchant. His business may prosper, and he may earn a good deal of money. Later his business may fail and he may lose much more than he earned. Both earning money and losing it are God's assignment to him. If this brother has the full assurance that his circumstances come from God's assignment, he will be able to worship the Lord for His arrangement. Perhaps losing money will benefit him more than earning money, for through such a loss he may be perfected and built up.

Likewise, both illness and good health come from God as His assignment. We should all aspire to be healthy. But sometimes good health does not perfect us as much as a period of illness. Furthermore, when our health fails, we may be more inclined to pray than when we are in good health.

The first prerequisite to having no anxiety is to have the full assurance that all the sufferings we experience are God's assignment. What need is there to worry about things? God has assigned them to us. He knows what we need.

When I was very young, I read a story about a conversation between two sparrows who were talking about the sorrows and the worries common among human beings. One sparrow asked the other why people worry so much. The other sparrow answered, "I don't think they have a Father who cares for them like we do. We don't need to worry about anything because our Father takes care of us." Yes, our Father does care for us. But sometimes He sends us hardships and sufferings to serve in fulfilling our destiny to magnify Christ. We can be freed from worry, not because God has promised us a life without suffering but because we know that all our circumstances come to us as God's assignment. Paul did not care about life or death. He cared only that Christ would be magnified in him. He realized that every circumstance was for his good. This is the way to have no anxiety.

Why do certain saints worry about losing money? Simply because their desire is to have more money. Why are others anxious about their health? They are anxious because they are afraid to die. If we are ill, we need to declare, "Satan, what can you do to me? I am not worried about death. Death does not make me anxious. Rather, the possibility of dying gives me another opportunity to magnify Christ." Instead of fearing poverty, illness, or death, we should welcome them if God sends them to us. Then we shall have no anxiety, for we shall know that every circumstance is an assignment from our Father. This does not mean, however, that we should seek suffering for its own sake. We should not do things that will cause us to suffer. Those who are in business should seek to make money, and those who are employees should try to get a promotion. But if we lose money or even lose our job, we need not be anxious. Such a loss comes from God's assignment, and we need not be anxious about it.

A LIFE FULL OF FORBEARANCE
BUT WITHOUT ANXIETY

(6)

Scripture Reading: Phil. 4:4-7; 1 Thes. 5:16-18;
Job 1:20-22; 2 Cor. 4:16-17; 12:7-9

In this chapter and in the chapter following we shall consider many of the details and fine points regarding a life full of forbearance but without anxiety. In particular we shall consider the way to fulfill Paul's word in Philippians 4:6, "In nothing be anxious."

We have pointed out repeatedly that the subject of the book of Philippians is the experience of Christ. In the first three chapters of this Epistle, the standard of Paul's writing is very high. However, in chapter four, the concluding portion of this book, Paul seems to descend to a lower level in emphasizing forbearance and anxiety.

More than fifty years ago, I was troubled by Philippians 4. I appreciated Paul's words in the first three chapters. In chapter one we see that we should magnify Christ by living Him; in chapter two, that we should take Christ as the pattern of the Christian life; and in chapter three, that Christ is far superior to all things of religion and culture and that we must count all things loss in order to pursue Him and gain Him. Then in chapter four Paul suddenly talks about forbearance and anxiety. I realized that forbearance was a virtue, but in my opinion Paul's word about forbearance could not compare with what he had written in the three previous chapters. Furthermore, I was troubled by the fact that Paul emphasized anxiety. But in recent years the light on the issue of forbearance versus anxiety has gradually become brighter and brighter. Now I have a deep appreciation for Paul's words, "Let your forbearance be known to all men" (v. 5) and, "In nothing be anxious" (v. 6).

TWO LIVES

Anxiety is the totality of the natural human life. Day by day and even hour by hour, the common human life is filled with anxiety. Every normal human being is anxious. The more sober you are in mind, the more anxious you will be. If you are a person who is thoughtful and careful, you will have a great deal of anxiety. Sensitive people are especially bothered by anxiety. Those who are unusually dull or insensitive may not have much anxiety, but those who are sensitive usually have many anxieties.

Just as anxiety is the totality of common human life, so forbearance is the totality of the proper Christian life. Hence, the words *anxiety* and *forbearance* represent two kinds of lives. Among human beings there are only two kinds of lives: the human life and the Christian life. Human life is a life of anxiety, whereas the Christian life is a life of forbearance. If we see this contrast, we shall realize that it is a matter of great importance for Paul to emphasize forbearance and anxiety in chapter four of Philippians. He emphasizes forbearance and anxiety because they represent two different kinds of lives. Every human being is subject to anxiety. But if we are a Christian according to the divine standard, we shall have a life full of forbearance and without anxiety. The first point I would emphasize in this chapter is that forbearance and anxiety represent two kinds of lives.

TWO SOURCES

Second, forbearance comes from God, and anxiety comes from Satan. This means that forbearance and anxiety represent two different sources—God and Satan.

God, the Source of Forbearance

The source of forbearance is God. God gives us forbearance so that we may accomplish His purpose. God has a purpose with us individually, with our families, and with us in the church. In order to carry out God's purpose related to us, to our families, and to the church, we need forbearance. If we lack the all-inclusive virtue of forbearance, it will be impossible for us to fulfill God's purpose. This means it will not be possible for us to allow God to fulfill His purpose with us, with our family, and with the church.

God has a threefold purpose with every one of us. He has a purpose for us individually, a purpose for us in relation to our family, and a purpose for us in the church life. It is crucial for us to realize that God has such a threefold purpose concerning us. For the fulfillment of such a divine purpose, we need forbearance. Without forbearance we shall not allow God to fulfill His purpose with us, with our family, or with the church.

We have seen that forbearance means to be utterly reasonable, considerate, and understanding in dealing with others. If we are forbearing, we shall have the wisdom and the ability to supply others with what they need. We shall also have the full knowledge of what to say to them and when to say it. For example, a parent who is forbearing will know how and when to speak to his children. If we do not exercise forbearance in our family life, we shall not be able to build up our family for the fulfillment of God's purpose. Not only is forbearance the totality of the proper Christian life; it is also the means given by God for the fulfillment of His threefold purpose with each of us. How precious that the source of forbearance is God! The forbearance we exercise and make known to others comes from God.

Satan, the Source of Anxiety

The source of anxiety is Satan. Anxiety comes from Satan to frustrate the fulfillment of God's purpose. Do not think that God assigns anxiety to us. In the foregoing chapter I said that anxiety comes from the circumstances assigned by God. To say that anxiety comes from God's assignment is quite different from saying that anxiety is God's assignment. Because of the fall, God has assigned sufferings to us. For example, God has ordained that women experience suffering in childbearing. He also ordained that men cope with thorns and thistles. Genesis 3:17-19, say, "Cursed is the ground for thy sake; in sorrow shalt thou eat of it all the days of thy life; thorns also and thistles shall it bring forth to thee...in the sweat of thy face shalt thou eat bread." Although God has assigned such sufferings, He has not assigned anxiety. After God made His assignment, Satan came in to cause anxiety through the sufferings assigned by God. Anxiety does not come from God. It comes from God's adversary, Satan, who uses the sufferings ordained by God to cause anxiety in human life. Therefore, anxiety comes from Satan and represents Satan, whereas forbearance comes from God and represents God.

How God Uses Satan

The Bible reveals that God uses Satan. We see this especially in the book of Job. When I first read this book, I was troubled by the fact that Satan had access to God's presence in the heavens. Job 1:6 says, "Now there was a day when the sons of God came to present themselves before the Lord, and Satan came also among them." The next verses record a conversation between God and Satan. I wondered how this conversation could take place. Why would God allow such an evil one to talk with Him? Why did He not destroy Satan, or at least drive him away? God used Satan to deal with Job. Job was righteous and perfect in himself; however, he did not truly know God. Thus, Job needed to be broken, to be dealt with thoroughly by God. God used Satan to accomplish this work, allowing Satan, within certain prescribed limits, to do certain things to Job.

From 2 Corinthians 12 we see that God also permitted a messenger from Satan to afflict Paul. Paul realized that his thorn in the flesh came from Satan. He says, "And lest I should be exalted above measure through the abundance of the revelations, there was given to me a thorn in the flesh, the messenger of Satan to buffet me, lest I should be exalted above measure" (v. 7). The principle is the same both in the case of Paul and of Job. Just as Satan was permitted by God to afflict Paul, he was allowed to afflict Job.

According to the first chapter of the book of Job, soon after Satan received permission to afflict Job, he sent calamities.

First, a report came that the Sabeans had stolen the oxen and the asses and slain the servants (Job 1:14-15). Immediately the report came of another calamity: fire had fallen from heaven and had consumed Job's sheep and other of his servants. Then the report came about the Chaldeans who stole the camels and slew still other servants. Then the news came of the fourth calamity: a "great wind from the wilderness" destroyed the house where Job's sons and daughters were feasting, and they all were killed. Here we see that Satan is able to use people, fire, and wind to bring in great destruction. When I first read Job 1, I did not understand why God allowed Satan to do such things. First Satan sends the calamities. Then he comes to cause anxiety.

God had a purpose in permitting Satan to afflict Job. God's purpose was to break Job, who was a perfect and self-righteous person. God used Satan to do what no human being was able to do. Since Job's friends could not deal with him, God used Satan for this task. Often the devil accomplishes certain difficult assignments for God. Sometimes if God cannot get through by using other people, He will permit Satan to deal with you. Concerning Job, God's purpose was to break him. Concerning Paul, God's purpose in allowing Satan to send a messenger to afflict his body was to keep him from being proud because of the visions and revelations he received. No doubt, Satan's purpose is always to attack God's people. This purpose is negative. But in permitting a satanic attack to take place, God has another purpose, a very positive one. All the sufferings we undergo are assigned to us by God for a positive purpose.

Paul speaks of this purpose in 2 Corinthians 4:16 and 17: "For which cause we faint not; but though our outward man is being consumed, yet the inward man is being renewed day by day. For the momentary lightness of the affliction worketh for us a far more exceeding and eternal weight of glory" (lit.). Although the afflictions are assigned by God, they do not come from Him directly. Rather, every affliction, disaster, calamity, or catastrophe comes from Satan. But they come with God's permission and for His purpose to perfect us. This was the reason Paul could declare that the present lightness of affliction works for us an exceeding weight of glory. God has a purpose to fulfill concerning us, and this purpose sometimes requires Satan's help.

A few months ago I had a problem with my health. I knew this problem was caused by the devil, Satan. But I also realized that it was permitted by God for a purpose. The Lord wanted to touch something in me, and He used this means to do it.

If we look at the cases of Job and Paul, we shall see that God permits Satan to cause affliction. As soon as the affliction comes, Satan comes to cause anxiety. The anxiety caused by Satan is for the frustration of God's purpose. To repeat, forbearance comes from God for the fulfillment of His purpose, but anxiety comes from Satan for the frustration of God's purpose. If we see this, we shall realize that it is not an insignificant matter for Paul to speak of forbearance and anxiety together in Philippians 4:5 and 6.

NO COEXISTENCE OF FORBEARANCE AND ANXIETY

If we have forbearance, we shall not have anxiety. But if we have anxiety, we shall not have forbearance. Just as God and Satan cannot stand together, so forbearance and anxiety cannot coexist. Whenever forbearance comes, anxiety must go. But if anxiety is with us, we shall be utterly lacking in forbearance. No one who exercises forbearance can be anxious. But if you are not a forbearing person, you will be anxious and filled with worry.

From experience, not from doctrine, we have come to understand that when we exercise forbearance in full, all anxiety disappears. If by God's mercy and grace we forbear with everyone, everything, and every matter, we shall not be anxious in anything. By God's mercy and grace we need to forbear with persons, things, and matters. If we are forbearing in this way, we shall not be subject to anxiety.

LIVING CHRIST AS OUR FORBEARANCE

We have seen that forbearance is actually Christ Himself lived out of us. The Christ in Philippians 1, 2, and 3 is the very forbearance Paul speaks of in 4:5. Thus, to make our forbearance known is to make our Christ known. Forbearance is actually the magnification of Christ. In 1:20 Paul says that Christ will be magnified in him, but in 4:5 he tells us to let our forbearance be known. When we put these verses together, we see that to let our Christ be magnified is to let our forbearance be known. Therefore, in our experience forbearance is Christ Himself.

If we live Christ as our forbearance, it will not be possible for us to be anxious. Anxiety is an impossibility for those who have Christ as their forbearance. Do you know why we are anxious and why we worry? We are anxious and worried because we do not live Christ. The words *live Christ* may merely be a doctrinal term, a way of speaking, not our actual living in a practical way. But when we live Christ day by day, anxiety has no ground within us.

I repeat, to forbear is to live Christ. In such a life, a life of forbearing everything by the grace of God, there is no room for anxiety. When we magnify Christ by living Him, anxiety has no way to touch us. Then because we live Christ as our forbearance, we shall be anxious for nothing.

A LIFE FULL OF FORBEARANCE
BUT WITHOUT ANXIETY

(7)

Scripture Reading: Phil. 4:4-7; 1 Thes. 5:16-18;
2 Cor. 12:7-9

In the foregoing chapter we pointed out that forbearance and anxiety represent two kinds of life, that forbearance comes from God and anxiety comes from Satan, and that forbearance and anxiety cannot coexist. Furthermore, we saw that to live Christ as our forbearance is to have a life free from anxiety. Now in this chapter we shall consider some further matters related to a life full of forbearance but without anxiety.

ONE WITH THE LORD

If we live Christ, we are truly one with the Lord. In Philippians 4:4 Paul says, "Rejoice in the Lord always; again I will say, rejoice." To rejoice in the Lord is to be one with Him. When we are one with the Lord, we are not anxious about anything, for we are not only under the Lord's sovereign hand, but we are in the Lord Himself. If we live this kind of life, how could we be anxious? The more we practice being one with the Lord, the more we shall realize that His destiny is our destiny. If He wants us to stay on earth for a longer period of time, He will keep us alive. But if it is His desire that we go to Him, He will take us to Himself. Since everything depends on His will and since we are one with Him in a practical way, there is no reason for us to be anxious.

When we are separated from the Lord, we are anxious

about everything. Everything in human life gives rise to anxiety. But when we are one with the Lord, we are separated from the natural human life and its anxiety. If we would make our forbearance known to all men and not be anxious in anything, we need to practice being one with the Lord. This is the reason Paul charges us to rejoice in the Lord before he exhorts us to make known our forbearance.

When I had a problem with my health a few months ago, I was bothered. One day the Lord checked with me and asked me if I was one with Him. When I said that I was one with Him, it was as if He said, "Since you are one with Me, you should not be anxious about your health."

We become anxious whenever we are not one with the Lord in a practical way. Doctrinally speaking, we are always one with Him. However, quite often we are not one with Him in practice. We may give messages to the saints, telling them that we are one spirit with the Lord. But in our daily living we need to be tested to see if we have the actual experience. If we are one with the Lord actually and practically, we shall not be anxious.

Even though Paul was a prisoner in Rome, he was not anxious about anything, because he was one with the Lord actually, practically, and thoroughly. He could even say that to die was better than to live. Paul was so one with the Lord that he knew that the Lord was his destiny. Not only was Paul's destiny in the hand of the Lord—his destiny was the Lord Himself. Because Paul was one with the Lord, he knew that Satan could not do anything to him, even though he might send a messenger, a thorn in the flesh, to buffet him. Paul was not worried about what Satan might do, for the Lord was his destiny.

THE SECRET OF SATISFACTION

If we are truly one with the Lord in our experience and something negative happens to us, we need not be anxious or troubled. If we are not one with the Lord in a practical way, virtually every person, every matter, and every thing will bother us. We may be disturbed by our husband or wife or by our children. When we are not one with the Lord, nothing will be satisfactory to us. For example, apart from the Lord, no job is satisfying. The secret of satisfaction is to be one with Christ. When we are one with the Lord, we can be satisfied with our circumstances, and we can be forbearing with everyone, every thing, and every matter. Only when we are one with Christ can we be forbearing to the uttermost and be satisfied in all situations.

If we would not have any anxiety, we must recognize that all afflictions, sufferings, calamities, disasters, and catastrophes are assigned by God. We also must be one with the Lord in our experience. Yes, we may realize the necessity of passing through suffering and affliction. But if we would be free from anxiety, we need something more than this realization. We must also be one with the Lord. Otherwise, eventually our circumstances or the things which happen to us will cause anxiety, and we shall not be satisfied with anything or anyone.

The older a person becomes, the more difficult it is for him to be satisfied. Throughout the years I have observed a good number of elderly persons who did not have Christ. The older they were, the more dissatisfied they became. Some were disgusted with almost everything and everyone. If we do not practice being one with the Lord, our situation will also become worse as we grow older. Out of a feeling of dissatisfaction, we may blame our circumstances or the members of our family. It is easy to satisfy a child or a young person, but difficult to satisfy someone who is older. This fact should motivate us to be one with the Lord in a practical way that we may be free from anxiety and have a life of forbearance.

PRAYER AND PETITION WITH THANKSGIVING

In 4:6 and 7 Paul says, "In nothing be anxious, but in everything, by prayer and petition with thanksgiving, let your requests be made known to God; and the peace of God, which surpasses all understanding, will guard your hearts and your thoughts in Christ Jesus." Paul certainly composed these verses in a very thoughtful way. In verse 6 he speaks of prayer, petition, and thanksgiving. Prayer is general and includes the essence of worship and fellowship; petition is special and is related to particular needs. According to Christian experience, to pray is to have fellowship, communion, with the Lord and to worship Him. Daily we need to have a time to contact the Lord, to have fellowship with Him, and to worship Him. During the course of our fellowship, we may have particular requests. Thus, we not only pray in a general way, but make petitions to the Lord in a particular way. We offer our petitions to the One with whom we are having fellowship. Petition, therefore, is a special request made during the course of our prayer.

It is significant that in 4:6 Paul does not speak of prayer, petition, *and* thanksgiving, but of prayer and petition *with* thanksgiving. Both our prayer and petition should be accompanied by thanksgiving to the Lord. Recently I once again learned the lesson of being thankful to the Lord. When I asked the Lord to restore my health, I was rebuked by Him for not thanking Him for the measure of health I still had. Whenever we are ill, we need to say, "Lord, I thank You that I am still healthy to a certain degree. Lord, I am ill, but I am not so ill that I cannot minister Christ to the saints. But, Lord, You know that I am not altogether healthy. Therefore, I ask You to improve my health and make me fully healthy again." We all need to learn to petition the Lord in this way.

Suppose a brother prays that the Lord will change his wife. If he prays in this way, the Lord may ask him why he does not offer thanks for his wife. Then the brother should pray, "Lord, I thank You for giving me a good wife." After offering thanks to the Lord, he then may proceed to ask Him to transform his wife.

Another brother may lose his job and pray to the Lord concerning employment. Instead of saying, "Lord, I have lost my job and I need You to have mercy on me," he should first thank the Lord. Perhaps he should say, "Lord, I thank You that I did not lose this job before now. Lord, I also thank You for the means I still have to support my family. O Lord, I have many things for which to thank You." Then along with his thanksgiving, he may ask the Lord to give him another job. But even as he prays concerning a new job, he should still be thankful and say, "Lord, I believe that You will give me a new job. Lord, You know what I need. I even thank You ahead of time for the job You will give me."

Let us all learn to pray and petition with thanksgiving. If we are thankful to the Lord, this will keep us from anxiety. But if we pray to the Lord out of worry, our anxiety will increase. Praying about our situation may actually cause our anxiety to grow. But if we pray and petition with thanksgiving, our anxiety will be driven away.

I must testify that I have learned to pray and petition with thanksgiving not from doctrine, but from my experience with the Lord. When I was ill recently, the Lord did rebuke me for not thanking Him. He reminded me that I am still healthy enough to function by releasing the Word. He rebuked me for allowing a little illness to disturb me and for complaining about my situation instead of exercising forbearance. By rebuking me for not thanking Him sufficiently, the Lord helped me to be satisfied in Him and not to be anxious. I thank the Lord for this training, which has come through a time of illness and through the Lord's rebuke.

ACCEPTING THE LORD'S WILL

Experiencing His Sufficient Grace

We have seen that to overcome anxiety we need to pray and have fellowship with the Lord and worship Him. Then with thanksgiving we need to make our petitions known. When we do this, we may think that the Lord will always answer us and give us what we ask. However, sometimes the Lord will say no. Consider Paul's experience of the thorn in the flesh. In 2 Corinthians 12:8 he says, "For this thing I besought the Lord thrice, that it might depart from me." However, the Lord denied Paul's request, and said to him, "My grace is sufficient for thee: for my strength is made perfect in weakness" (v. 9). Therefore, Paul could declare, "Most gladly therefore will I rather glory in my infirmities, that the power of Christ may rest upon me." The crucial point here is that Paul accepted the will of God. He realized that God's will was to leave the thorn with him so that he could experience His sufficient grace. Because Paul accepted the Lord's will, he did not have any anxiety.

Yes, we need to pray and petition the Lord with thanksgiving. But when the Lord does not grant our petition, our anxiety may increase instead of decrease. At such a time, we realize that the Lord will not change our situation. Instead, He allows the "thorn" to remain. He knows that we need the thorn. He also needs it that He may reveal His sufficient grace and in addition train us to trust in Him. If we do not accept the Lord's will but insist on making petitions according to our own will, we shall not be able to escape anxiety.

Suppose you pray to the Lord when you are suffering from a certain illness. The Lord may answer your prayer and heal you. He does this especially on behalf of those who are rather young in their experience of Him. At a later time, however, you may again become sick and ask the Lord to heal you. Instead of healing you suddenly, He may heal you gradually, or He may not heal you at all. Eventually, it may become clear to you that the Lord intends for the illness to remain. If you accept His will in the matter, you will be at peace. You will not have any anxiety.

When Brother Nee was a young man, he suffered from heart disease. Often when he ministered the Word he was in such pain that he had to lean on a stand for support. Although he contracted this disease before he was thirty years of age, he lived with that illness for nearly forty years. Although he knew that he could die from that disease at any time, he accepted the Lord's will and was not anxious. He realized that his illness was a thorn given him for the fulfillment of God's purpose.

Trusting the Lord

Accepting the Lord's will in particular matters not only enables us to experience His sufficient grace; it also teaches us to have a life of trusting the Lord. If the thorn had been taken away from Paul, Paul probably would not have trusted in the Lord as much as he did with the thorn. Simply because the thorn was allowed to remain, day by day Paul had to live a life of trusting in the Lord.

We all prefer that hardships and sufferings be taken away from us. But sometimes the Lord will say, "No, I cannot answer your request. It is better for this thing to remain so that you may learn to trust Me and not be anxious." If we accept the Lord's will and trust Him, we shall not be anxious. However, if we do not accept His will or if we do not live by trusting in Him, we shall be anxious.

According to my natural life, I am the kind of person who likes everything to be perfect. If I become ill in some way, my desire is to be healed thoroughly. Even if there is something wrong with an article of clothing, I want it fixed and made perfect. I want everything under my management to be right in every way. But I cannot control whether or not sickness comes to me. The Lord may assign illness to me, realizing that I need it so that I may learn to trust Him and not worry. For this I need to say, "Lord, I thank You that this sickness is a help to me. I also thank You, Lord, that even this fulfills Your purpose." The more we thank the Lord in this way, the more we shall have forbearance in place of anxiety.

A PROPER REALIZATION

Whether or not we can exercise forbearance in difficult situations depends on the kind of realization and practice we have. If we realize that a particular situation is of the Lord, that it is needed to perfect us, and then thank Him for it, we shall not be anxious or threatened. We shall be able to say, "Lord, I thank You for this. I am not threatened by this thing, because I know that I am one with You and that everything which comes to me is Your assignment. Lord, I also know that You allow this thing to remain that it may help You to fulfill Your purpose and to perfect me." If we realize that everything is the Lord's assignment and if we accept His will and thank Him for it, we shall be able to say with Paul, "For which cause we faint not; but though our outward man is consumed, yet the inward man is being renewed day by day. For the momentary lightness of the affliction worketh for us a far more exceeding and eternal weight of glory" (2 Cor. 4:16-17, lit.). Then we shall not have any anxiety.

Christians often say that the way to be freed from anxiety

is simply to believe in the Lord. According to this understanding, the fact that a person is anxious means that he does not
believe in the Lord. However, in 4:6 Paul does not say that it
is by believing that we do not have anxiety in anything. In
this context he does not say a word about believing.

SIX POINTS TO UNDERSTAND AND PRACTICE

If we would be free from anxiety, we need to understand
and practice the six points we have covered in the foregoing
chapter and in this chapter. First, we need to realize that just
as anxiety is the totality of human life, so forbearance is the
totality of the Christian life. Second, we need to see that the
source of forbearance is God and that the source of anxiety is
Satan.

The third matter is to realize that forbearance and anxiety cannot exist together. The reason for this is that forbearance is actually a person, Christ Himself. Only when Christ is
lived out of us do we have forbearance. This is indicated by
the fact that in Philippians 1, 2, and 3 Paul speaks of Christ
again and again. He emphasizes magnifying Christ, taking
Christ as our pattern, and pursuing Christ as our goal. But in
Philippians 4 he uses the term forbearance and charges us to
make our forbearance known to all men. Actually, this forbearance is the very Christ revealed in the foregoing chapters. Therefore, to let our forbearance be known is to live
Christ.

We have seen that God may assign certain sufferings to us.
But although the sufferings are God's assignment, they do
not come from God, but from Satan. The experiences of both
Job and Paul illustrate this. The calamities assigned to us by
God actually come to us from Satan. Satan is the messenger
who brings these things to us. God assigned a certain thorn to
Paul, and He permitted Satan to bring the thorn to him.
Immediately after sending us a certain difficulty or affliction,
Satan comes to cause anxiety. This anxiety is not assigned by
God and it does not come from Him. On the contrary, it is
always caused by Satan to frustrate God's purpose. If we have
a full realization of this, we shall see the need for Christ as
our forbearance. If we have this forbearance, we shall not

have anxiety. But if we have anxiety, we shall not have forbearance.

The fourth matter we need to understand and exercise is
that to have a life full of forbearance but without anxiety, we
need to be one with the Lord in a practical way. To be one with
the Lord experientially is to be in Him.

Fifth, we need to pray. This means we need to have a time
of fellowship with the Lord and to worship Him. Prayer does
not mean merely to ask the Lord for things. Prayer involves
conversing with the Lord, communicating with Him in fellowship, and worshipping Him. As we spend time with the Lord
in this way, we should make known our petitions with thanksgiving.

Sixth, after praying, having fellowship with the Lord, worshipping Him, and making our petitions known to Him, we
shall know what the will of the Lord is. For example, if we are
ill, we shall know whether the Lord intends to heal us or
allow the sickness to remain. Once we know God's will, we
should accept it, experience His sufficient grace, trust in Him,
and thank Him. Then we shall have a life full of forbearance
but without anxiety.

**Additional Information
on the Life-study of Philippians**

All sixty-two messages from the
Life-Study of Philippians
are available for reading online
at www.ministrybooks.org.

Printed editions of this series can be ordered
from Living Stream Ministry
by telephone (1-800-549-5164)
or online at www.livingstream.com.

Electronic editions of this series
for hand-held devices can be ordered online
from Living Stream Ministry
at http://www.lsm.org/epublications.html.

Additional Distribution Information

This free publication is distributed by Bibles for America and its affiliates in Australia, New Zealand, and Canada. All are non-profit organizations dedicated to the spread and understanding of the Word of God. For additional information, you may contact us at:

Bibles for America
P. O. Box 17537
Irvine, CA 92623
USA
Toll free: 1.888.551.0102
info@biblesforamerica.org
www.biblesforamerica.org

Bibles for Australia
P. O. Box 8174
Burwood Heights 3151, Victoria
Australia
Toll free: 1800 008 775
info@biblesforaustralia.org.au
www.biblesforaustralia.org.au

Bibles for New Zealand
P. O. Box 302746
North Harbour
Auckland 0751
New Zealand
Toll free: 0800 40 40 80
info@biblesfornewzealand.org.nz
www.biblesfornewzealand.org.nz

Bibles for Canada
P. O. Box 71088 RPO Silver Springs
Calgary AB T3B 5K2
Canada
Toll free: 1-877-232-5933
info@biblesforcanada.org
www.biblesforcanada.org